QUIT IS NOT AN OPTION

THE ACT OF LOVE, CARING, AND NOT QUITTING
TERRY HAYWOOD

S.H.E. PUBLISHING, LLC

QUIT IS NOT AN OPTION
The Act of Love, Caring, and Not Quitting

Copyright © 2024 by Terry Haywood

All rights reserved. Printed in the United States of America. No part of this book may be used or reproduced in any manner whatsoever without written permission except in the case of brief quotations embodied in critical articles or reviews.

For information contact:

www.shepublishingllc.com | info@shepublishingllc.com

Cover and Title Page Design by Nabin

Library of Congress Control Number: 2024947220

ISBN:
978-1-964061-17-7 (paperback)
978-1-964061-18-4 (hardback)
First Edition: November 2024

10 9 8 7 6 5 4 3 2 1

Table of Contents

Impossible or Not? 1
God's Plan 3
When Quit Was No Option 2012—2013 7
Understanding Not to Quit 15
Still No Quit 21
Teamwork—Not to Quit 25
Wannabe Athlete 31
Why Quit Hurts 37
Becoming a Man 41
When Terry Met Donna 43
Living Life as a Comedian 51

From the moment we are born until eternity, we may encounter unexpected, life-changing events. But what happens when an event is so devastating, so unusual, that it seems impossible to endure? What do we do? How do we adjust? How do we come to accept the "impossible"?

Impossible or Not?

Living by the words of the late and great Nelson Mandela: "It only seems impossible until it's done," I accepted the challenge of the "impossible"—being a caregiver.

I am Terry Haywood, Sr., a sixty-four-year-old man who has been devoted to providing the best care for my wife, Donna, for over eleven years. We have been married for more than thirty-eight years.

God's Plan

Stories are often told about how we turn to God in times of need. Confession: I did too. Without doing so, I might now be facing countless challenges, making poor decisions, and struggling through life's difficult moments.

I often wondered to myself, "Has God given up on me?" "Does God still care?"

What I discovered was that God had been with me all along, since the very beginning—February 21, 1960, at 3:45 a.m., when I was born to a strong, loving, and resilient single mother and a father who abandoned his responsibilities. Although my life could have turned out much better, it could also have been much worse. Today, I am at peace, sharing my life with the woman I have loved since 1982.

My moment of solace came at fifty-five when I finally understood why God had brought this woman into my life. She not only loved and supported me but also married me and became my partner for two-thirds of my life—someone I cannot live without, not even for a day. Only God knows the many roads I traveled to find her.

To reach this point, however, I had to learn to take responsibility for my life before I met her. That included embracing my unwavering love for my son, Terry Jr., who was born out of love from a previous relationship. I had to understand that my son would always be my responsibility, no matter where he is or how old he becomes, for as long as I live. Being a man is a 24/7 job—and I love the hours.

Caring for someone you love, especially your spouse, can be one of life's greatest tasks. My wife was only 52 years old in November 2012 when life-changing events occurred. Supporting her during that time required a strong network of trusted people. The most important lesson I learned on this "impossible" journey was the immense value of family, friends, and professionals. Although I cannot recall all their names, I will always remember their presence and the impact they had on our lives.

Still, love can hurt, and caregiving is both emotionally and financially demanding. It requires an abundance of mental strength and resources. Currently, I see a therapist to process my emotions and improve both my mental and physical health. I urge men and women alike to listen to their bodies and care for themselves in addition to caring for their loved ones.

We must also remember that money is not everything. We need to learn to control money rather than let it control us. Life is worth far more than a few dollars. So, seek help when needed. As the saying goes, "We don't know until we don't know." Taking care of our mental health enables us to better care for others.

When Quit Was No Option
2012—2013

Most people would be thankful on the day after Thanksgiving. They would probably be reflecting on fabulous meals shared with family, friends, and maybe even individuals they wished were elsewhere. Unfortunately, Donna and I were facing the "impossible" in the worst way imaginable. We were not thankful. Instead, the impossible stared at us like an angry bull that had a bad day at the rodeo.

Just one day after Thanksgiving in 2012, Donna suffered her second stroke—of what would eventually become three. That day, she became unresponsive and withdrawn, barely able to make sense of her surroundings. The warning signs had appeared about a week earlier: Donna was unusually tired, had stopped participating in activities she loved—like bowling, buying lottery tickets, and enjoying life. She had never missed a day of work or bowling, but she had now missed five consecutive days of work.

In a life-saving moment, I called 911. Donna was rushed to Loyola University Hospital in Maywood, Illinois, just a few miles southeast of Bellwood, where we had built a happy life in our Georgian home since February 1991. It was on that cold, dark, and frightful night, at just fifty-two years old, that she suffered her second stroke.

Donna had always been a great athlete in bowling, track, volleyball, and softball. But the excessive cigarette smoking and the stress of being laid off from her job of over ten years at Marsh had taken a toll on her. It was too much for her body to handle.

When Donna was admitted to the ICU, family and friends flocked to her side. For the first two weeks, her room was filled with overwhelming support from my mom, Christine (RIP 2/9/24, with tears in my eyes and love in my heart), family, friends, bowlers, and coworkers. However, as time passed, many of them slowly drifted away. But true family and friends never quit.

Donna's dad, Earl, her mom, Donnie, and her older brother, Michael, had passed away more than thirty years ago. Donnie had been an active member of the Blessed Sacrament Church at the corner of Cermak and Central Park. Since 1993, Donna had relied on me, our extended family, and close friends.

As the days went by, uncertainty grew. Donna was in a "touch-and-go" situation, and I feared I might lose her. I was terrified. In that moment, I did what any strong man would do—I cried. I cried seeing my wife, my best friend, my soulmate lying motionless in a hospital bed, completely helpless. I cried so much that I had to leave her room and sit in the waiting area.

It was there that a chaplain introduced herself to me. She offered prayer services for those of the Catholic faith and asked if she could pray with me. Although I am Baptist and hadn't reached out to God in a long time, I agreed. I was ashamed to admit how distant I had become from God. But on that day, I decided it was time to let God know how I felt about Donna and my commitment to her. If given the opportunity, I vowed to be by her side until the day my heart stopped beating.

That was the moment *Quit Is Not an Option!* began.

With Donna unconscious, I prayed with the chaplain. This time, my prayers weren't about trivial things, like asking for a bike as a kid or avoiding a test in school. They weren't even entirely about me—though maybe just a little. My prayers were for Donna's health. I asked God to challenge me, to test me, because taking care of Donna would be my "impossible," and I was determined to rise to the challenge.

Donna was transferred to intensive care, and it was like a scene from a horror movie—alarms blaring, people rushing everywhere. The hospital staff expressed concern that Donna needed rest, as visitors were becoming a major distraction. By the time night turned to day, the large crowd had dwindled to just me, alone with my thoughts.

This was Donna's second stroke, the first having occurred in 2003. That year, she was admitted to Northwestern Hospital in Downtown Chicago. It was the same year as the infamous Chicago Cubs playoff game when Steve Bartman reached over the wall and interfered with a foul ball. Now, in 2012, here I was in the hospital again, battling fears that this time might be worse.

My thoughts were a whirlwind. At first, I was positive: *"Donna will be okay! She'll recover in a few days!"* Then darker thoughts crept in: *"Am I going to be a widower at fifty-two?"* I prayed. I cried. It was all I could do.

On the second day, I went home to handle practical matters—calling Donna's job to inform them of her condition and regretfully explaining that she would no longer be able to work. Donna had only been at her dream job with Allied Worldwide for about a year after searching for employment for so long. Losing it felt like an unbearable blow.

When I returned to the hospital, alarms were going off near Donna's room. My heart sank as I realized the commotion was coming from her room. Doctors and nurses were working feverishly to save her. When they were done, the doctor told me, "Donna will not walk, talk, or see again."

A friend, Elanor, visited Donna and encouraged me not to accept the doctor's prognosis. She reminded me to stay hopeful, pray, and take care of myself because Donna needed me to be strong. It took time, but I learned.

Caring for myself became a priority—sleep, water, food, and exercise were vital. I also reminded myself that I couldn't save the world, so I stopped trying. Stress does terrible things to the body, and life is too short to make it shorter.

On the fourth day, a miracle happened. Walking into Donna's room, I saw her sitting up, smiling—the brightest smile I had seen in years. She looked at the nurse, pointed at me, and said, "There's my Boo-Boo!" That moment was bittersweet. My wife was awake, and though I had no idea where "Boo-Boo" came from, it didn't matter. She was alive.

Even now, twelve years later, I cherish being Donna's caregiver. When she smiles, I smile. When she hurts, I hurt. And I will continue to do everything in my power to care for her because that's what love means.

Understanding Not to Quit

In December 2012, Donna was admitted to the Lexington rehabilitation center in LaGrange, IL, where she stayed for six months regaining her strength and relearning basic skills like eating, drinking, and bathing.

During her time there, Donna accepted, adjusted to, and embraced her new normal. Unfortunately, adjusting to rehab food was tough at first; she had to eat liquid meals. For someone who loved seven-course meals, this was a frustrating change. She would complain, curse, and even conspire to sneak food in. Guess who helped her with that? (Tip: sneaking food into rehab is not a good idea—for patients or visitors!) Thankfully, after a couple of weeks, Donna was back to eating regular food, which at least made that part of her stay better. With the help of several therapists and extensive effort, she was able to come home around April 2013.

As her husband, accepting our new normal has been, and still is, my toughest challenge. The key is knowing that no matter how much we cry, plead, or pray, the sooner we accept our reality, the better life becomes. In addition, we must set realistic goals for improvement. This is where support and understanding are vital. Our loved ones are adjusting to even greater challenges, so we must be patient and empathetic—they are not us, and we are not them.

Time heals most wounds, and adjusting becomes easier. I hold onto the hope that Donna will one day walk again. For now, I ask for smaller miracles, like being able to stand again, and then we'll focus on walking. This experience has been life-changing for both of us, and I've learned that the quicker we adjust, the sooner life moves forward.

Since we live in a two-story home, Donna hasn't been able to access the second floor independently. She stays on the first floor for now, but her goal is to climb those stairs one day. She cried when she fell trying to walk for the first time, and she's experienced memory issues, forgetting certain events or names. Interestingly, Donna remembers events from before 2012 with remarkable clarity and can even elaborate on them—including the occasional fib I told (kidding!). For someone who has survived three strokes, congestive heart failure, a heart attack, several emergency room visits, and COVID-19 twice, her memory is truly remarkable. Reflecting on her life, Donna only ever took one sick day during her thirty-plus-year career.

"How do I adjust to all of this?" I asked myself. "What happened to Donna?" In the beginning, it felt like there was no end in sight. Everything bad was happening, and I was overwhelmed with emotions. I was angry—angry at family, friends, work, life. But none of these people had done anything wrong. I realized I had to quit. Yes, *quit*. I had to quit feeling sorry for myself and start keeping my promise to care for Donna. Seeing life through a glass half full felt impossible, but I knew I had to try.

From 2015 to 2020, we hit rock bottom. Donna was hospitalized in 2015, 2018, and 2020—each time around the holidays. It seemed like we spent more time with Santa than with family. Each hospitalization brought uncertainty, rehab, and setbacks. To make matters worse, we both caught COVID-19. Our prayers go out to those who lost loved ones during one of the most severe pandemics in history.

Despite everything, quitting was not an option. We made adjustments to our home to make life easier, such as installing a home monitor to check on Donna when I'm in another room or outside. Still, it's hard for me to leave her, even for a quick trip to the store. Yet Donna remains strong and positive, still managing to boss me around as she's done since the day we said, "I do."

Today, Donna is wheelchair-bound but can stand for a few seconds. We rely on DoorDash for groceries because we don't travel much. Donna enjoys watching her beloved White Sox on TV. Though she no longer attends games like she did with her father, she cheers (or boos) from home.

Her custom-made jersey, featuring her old softball number, 9, brings her joy.

    I've learned to accept that Donna didn't ask for her situation. Despite her medical setbacks, she's never asked, "Why me?" In fact, she's the one who comforts me when I'm upset, often calling me a "big baby." I love her honesty. We've built a relationship on open communication and mutual support, which is essential for navigating this journey together.

Still No Quit

Each morning, afternoon, evening, and night, Donna needs to take several medications. I must ensure she stays on schedule and record her vitals to provide updates to her doctors. At first, I was nervous: "What if she takes the wrong medicine?" "What if I give her too much or not enough?" "What if I fall asleep?" However, I had to learn to establish routines to make it easier. I set up appointments with her doctors, dentist, and specialists.

I also started cooking—who else was going to do it? At first, we visited restaurants daily. Before her illness, Donna cooked meals fit for a king, which explains why my weight skyrocketed over those twenty-five years. But after her illness made it impossible for her to cook, I had to step up. I've been a student in the kitchen, learning fast and well. It's been twelve years, and Donna has yet to get sick from my cooking!

My goal is to be a "chief" in the kitchen. The only difference between *chef* and *chief* is "I." Learning to cook has been fun, especially since Donna wouldn't eat my cooking before—or would pretend to! I still remember the time I made eggs and bacon for her; they must have been awful because I found them in the garbage, still smoking hot. I never quit and only got better. Today, I'm making her my favorite dish: fish, greens, beans, mashed potatoes, and any other meat she desires.

The feeling I get when I see her eyes first thing in the morning—it's the start of a great day. I used to sleep on the floor next to her bed, which is on the first floor of our two-story home. Since her illness, Donna has been unable to climb the fourteen stairs to our bedroom. It's lonely up there without her.

Donna loves to bathe, and before 2012, she did it often. Now I help her with this routine, which includes her special Summer's Eve body wash, Sugar Berry perfume (which Donna calls "coconut spray"), beeswax lip balm, and Purell hand sanitizer—all in that order. It's her routine, and she sticks to it. Learning and honoring these little details means so much to her, and I try not to take them for granted. Additionally, I help with hair braiding and nail grooming whenever needed.

The toughest adjustment for Donna and me was transitioning to working a full-time job from home. From 1987 to 2020, I worked at CNA Insurance in downtown Chicago, commuting by car for thirty-one years and by train for two. From 2018 to 2020, I worked in the office from 9–1, rode the train home, and then worked from home from 3–7 to finish my workday. All the while, I cared for Donna during any remaining hours.

At first, balancing employment and caregiving was great. I was getting exercise, feeling productive, and maintaining my health. However, over time, my daily walk to the train station seemed longer and more grueling. The workweek felt like it stretched over eight days. In 2020, just as I was contemplating retirement, a bittersweet moment occurred: our offices shut down due to COVID-19. While the pandemic was devastating, it gave me the opportunity to work from home full-time. For the past three years, I've excelled at balancing remote work and caregiving.

Separating my roles as husband and caregiver has been the toughest challenge. Sometimes, my decisions aren't popular, and Donna may not understand them. When making these choices, I always prioritize her well-being and try to ensure she understands that I'm here to support her in the best way possible. We must allow our loved ones as much autonomy as possible, even when it's challenging. Everyone deserves the right to choose how they live—or die. While our intentions are good, it's crucial to step into the shoes of those we care for and remember how tough it is for them.

Donna, for example, loves her lottery games—Pick 3, Pick 4, Little and Big Lotto, and Powerball. If there's a lottery, Donna wants to play! But the lottery costs money, so sometimes it's just not possible to play. When her numbers do win, explaining why there's no payout is not a good feeling!

Teamwork—Not to Quit

I grew up in a modest but vibrant community in Chicago called Bronzeville. Our neighborhood was affectionately referred to as "39th!" It was located at the corners of 3900 South and Indiana Streets (200 East), where the famous Rothschild's liquor store has stood for over seventy years. Over time, Rothschild's transformed into a grocery, medicine, and lottery store.

Our community had barbecue joints, churches, local hardware stores, record shops, and resources like the Elliott Donnelly Youth Center of Chicago, which helped shape the lives of many less fortunate. The center, located at 3947 South Michigan Avenue next to the Chicago Transit train tracks, was a cornerstone of the neighborhood. I still remember when the L train derailed near 40th and State Street in the late 60s or early 70s. It took me a long time to feel comfortable riding trains again.

Programs like free school lunches and summer jobs made a big difference in our lives. I participated in any program I could, starting my first job in 1974 at the Firman House on 37 West 47th Street when I was just fourteen years old.

The mentors who gave their time and love were pivotal in our neighborhood. They kept many of us off the streets and out of trouble. I pray we return to a time when people cared for and respected each other more. The world is becoming cold, angry, and violent. Where is the love?

The people of Bronzeville in those early years set high standards for their children. Parents were parents to all the kids in the neighborhood. My mom, Christine, was key to my early development. She taught us to be appreciative and lived a remarkable eighty-six years, passing away on February 9, 2024. Sixty-four of those years were spent with me. As the oldest, I had the first opportunity to witness a strong, black, and beautiful woman set an example of resilience, kindness, and strength.

My mom came to Chicago from North Mississippi in the early 40s. Life there had to be tough for her. She arrived in Chicago with my uncle, W.D.—whom we affectionately called "Oots" or "Uncle Oots"—as a single, twenty-two-year-old mother with a son. I know very little about my biological father beyond his name. Later, Mom met John Aster Thomas, my stepfather and the biological father of my brothers, Tim and Darryl. Sadly, John passed away on April 6, 1976, at only fifty-eight years old. His death, from cancer, was devastating. As a sixteen-year-old, I lost my first male mentor.

Despite our challenges, my mom never allowed us to feel sorry for ourselves. She ensured we had food on the table and clothes on our backs. She used to say, "We ain't the Joneses, so don't try to be like them!" Our family valued competition in sports and life, and we were taught never to quit. Quitting was frowned upon, especially when money was spent on lessons or participation.

I developed a strong drive to succeed and set small goals, imagining where I wanted to be in five or ten years. Like many young Black men growing up in humble homes, I needed money, stability, support, and love. I was passionate about succeeding in life.

Growing up in Bronzeville also meant nicknames. Some of the best ones I remember from over fifty years ago include: Dad, Po-John, Goodtime Charlie, Hook, Oots, Rose, Doll, Tee, Sonny, Sweet, Sister, Mosconi, Eyes, Leen-Leen, Boxer, Bootsy, Popper, Cat, Netta, Girly, Boysee, and many more. As for me, I've been called "Fatboy" and "Dong" (pronounced Dooonggg). Those over fifty call me "Fatboy" because I was chubby as a kid, though today, at 5'8" and 163 pounds, I've long outgrown that nickname.

In honor of my mom, whom I lost earlier this year, I often refer to myself as Chris, Jr., the male version of my mom.

I started attending church and learning about God at nine years old. At the time, I was a student at Mayo Elementary on 37th and Giles. The dean of the school also served as a young pastor and held services in a small, cold church basement on 37th and Wabash, about two blocks from my school. I also attended Zion Grove Church on 39th and Prairie. Those experiences taught me valuable lessons about good, evil, and living by the Golden Rule.

Adulthood brought its challenges. Being an adult means juggling many responsibilities—children, jobs, parents, and life itself. Sometimes, life hits you hard, and you reach "rock bottom."

Although my biological father was absent, I always tried to maintain a strong relationship with my own son. On Father's Day 2023, I had a bittersweet moment when I learned my father's real name and some details about him. While celebrating my own role as a father, I also mourned the relationship I never had with my dad.

Bronzeville in the 70s was a tight-knit community where everyone knew you, your family, and your business. Today, we use social media to stay connected, and the Haywoods are no exception. Family will always be family, no matter where we are in the world.

Wannabe Athlete

My attitude was arrogant, childish, and terrible—I hated to lose at anything. My will to win became so intense that I remember being sent to bed because my mom felt I was too hard on my cousin during a card game we were losing. "He is only seven, Terry!" she yelled as she made me *quit* the game this time.

Before high school, I was known as a neighborhood legend—at least, that's what I believed. From baseball to basketball, football to hockey (yes, hockey), I played it all. At twelve years old, I was the tournament MVP in 1972 during a floor hockey tournament at BBR Youth Center on 16th and Hamlin in the Lawndale community on Chicago's West Side. I was such a competitor that, where I came from, second place was considered the first loser. I took that to heart.

I earned over forty-one trophies competing in tournaments throughout Chicago at places like the Chicago Boys Clubs, EDYC Youth Center,

Hyde Park Neighborhood Club, Lincoln Center, Dunbar, Pershing, Stateway, and Garfield Parks. You name it, I was there competing. However, since many of those trophies were for second or even third place, in my old neighborhood, I would have been credited with only twelve trophies. So, I keep the real count to myself.

As mentioned, I won many awards. However, I owe much of my success to the Elliot Donnelly Youth Center and its employees—basketball coaches William Boline and Ralph Clark, hockey coach Alonzo "Bear" Williams, and mentors Virginia "Jenny" Clayton and Jerome Washington. I also can't forget Lil Bil, the lifeguard at our swimming pool (our community had nicknames for everyone). Our youth center, located at 3947 South Michigan on the South Side of Chicago, was a lifeline for kids like me.

I spent most of my younger and teenage years there. It was a place where we met kids from different neighborhoods, learned how to play sports, cooked, received tutoring, and more. For a typical "underdog," as I like to call myself, youth centers like this kept me and other low-income kids from winding up in jail or worse. I give a big "thank you" to the Youth Centers of Chicago.

In 1968, as an eight-year-old, I learned teamwork and how to relate to people outside my family. Our biddy basketball team (for boys eight to twelve years old) lost its first two games to teams from competing youth centers: Chatham Y and Old Town Boys Club. The first game against Chatham ended with a humiliating score of 134–3. The local news even posted the score the next day. Our only question was, "Who scored the three points for us?"

The second game was closer—we lost 100–23. Despite the improvement, I quit. My excuse? "If I'm going to lose, it should at least be with some dignity!" Losing felt terrible. Today, I realize that with hard work, patience, and sometimes a good break, I might have been on the team winning games by scores like 134–3. Or at least I would have tried harder and not quit.

Fifty years later, I am reminded of those teammates when I think back to my mom's funeral service on February 24, 2024, at Zion Baptist Church.

Alan "Baba" Bowman was one of twelve twelve-year-olds to make the biddy basketball all-star team that went on to play in Puerto Rico. It was such a big deal that our elementary school, Mayo, held an Alan Bowman Day. I was so jealous back then. Why didn't they pick me? Today, I understand—I wasn't as good as Alan. In fact, no one in our school was. He was like a young Michael Jordan before Jordan became famous. Alan was also the left winger on our youth hockey team, where I played center.

Elliott "Big E" Hayes was our center in basketball and goalie on the hockey team. He was also my best friend, allowing me to share his family, especially his dad. I hadn't experienced sitting down at a family dinner table before, and I loved every minute of it. His family—father Thomas Sr., mom Alberta, brother Thomas Jr. ("Boop"), and sister Lucretia—became like my own.

Louis "Eyes" Haywood, my older cousin by five days, was the most improved athlete in the neighborhood. He became our best scorer, rebounder, and enforcer. Louis was pure-hearted, never drank or smoked, and never got into trouble.

Earl "Curly" Haywood joined our basketball team later but also played baseball on several teams. Unfortunately, a serious illness ended his athletic career, but he is alive and doing well today.

Kevin "KP" Pickens couldn't hit a baseball with a shovel, but he was my favorite person to be around. Like a young Kevin Hart, KP's personality boomed, and he has been happily married to his childhood sweetheart, Valerie Gray, for over thirty years.

James "Big Bro" Flemming was a mentor to many kids in our neighborhood. Seeing him at my mom's funeral meant the world to me. Though I didn't get the chance to thank him in person, I hope he reads this book and knows how much he is appreciated.

Ronnie Lester, aka Santo, played shortstop on the Black Cubs' team when I was nine years old.

Later, he became a standout basketball player at Dunbar High School.

Terry Cummings, aka TC, played for his neighborhood team at Altgeld Gardens and was destined for greatness. I still remember him blocking my layup and sending the ball nearly across the court. He was a terror to play against.

Glen "Doc" Rivers from Proviso East in Maywood, IL, played in a tournament at Lincoln Center. I still follow Doc as coach of the Milwaukee Bucks and wish him well (except when they play the Chicago Bulls!).

Good teamwork starts long before stepping onto the court. It takes practice, commitment, and camaraderie. Even fifty years later, our basketball team is still a team—now as well-adjusted men with families of our own.

Why Quit Hurts

In high school, I learned how decisions to quit or make poor choices could impact the way I live today. During my sophomore year at Dunbar Vocational, located on 30th and King Drive on the South Side of Chicago, I earned the starting shortstop position on the junior-varsity baseball team. I was so excited—I thought this was my opportunity to make it to the major leagues and earn millions of dollars. Or so I believed at the time.

Before the season began, all players were required to complete a physical exam. Unfortunately, due to limited medical resources, my results were delayed by a week. By the time the physical was submitted to the coach, I had been demoted to the backup shortstop position. How unfair, I thought. It wasn't even my fault, yet I was being benched!

On a bright, hot, breezy summer day in June 1976, I decided to *quit* the team during a game.

Why? Because I wasn't in the starting lineup and was warming the bench (a term we used for backup players). That's why! I thought I would show the coach who was boss.

The next day, I did just that—or so I thought. Not only was the coach the boss of the baseball team, but he was also my gym teacher and the dean of students. When Coach Gant, my coach/gym teacher/dean, saw me after I quit the baseball team, he was clearly disappointed. Not because I wasn't a good player, but because I had quit.

Instead of asking for a second chance, I had given up.

Coach Gant told me something I've never forgotten: "WINNERS NEVER QUIT, AND QUITTERS NEVER WIN!" Those words were permanently etched in my mind and heart that day.

Swimming was another challenge for me. I hated water! But to pass gym class, I had to swim across the shallow end of the pool—with Coach Gant watching, of course. I stood there, trembling with fear, staring at the cold, blue water in our high school's indoor swimming pool.

As I took on the task for the first (and only) time, Coach Gant shouted from the sidelines, "Come on, HAYWOOD, you can do it!" Somehow, I managed to cross the pool. Although it took time to recover—getting the water out of my stomach and changing into dry clothes—I made it!

Coach Gant's persistence and commitment to teaching me a life lesson made a lasting impression on how I view challenges like swimming.

Although I'm still no lifeguard, I've grown to enjoy water. I also recognize how important it is for young athletes to have someone like Coach Gant in their lives—someone who can teach lessons about perseverance and humility. Sometimes, hearing the truth can set us free, enabling us to grow and learn.

Becoming a Man

In July 1979, I met Gail Elissa Smith, "Bea," who would eventually become the mother of my only child—a son. She named him Terry Jr. (TJ) after me, saying that I was smart and she wanted our son to be like me. My only question was: How could I be considered smart when I was a twenty-year-old dad still living with my mom?

We moved into an apartment on the North Side of Chicago, across town from where I grew up. We got engaged and planned to get married, though we never set a date. Unfortunately, our time together was short-lived. We soon realized that the only thing we truly had in common was TJ. Looking back, we were just two young teens moving too fast, too soon. Our relationship lasted only two years.

After Gail and I split up, I moved back to Bronzeville with my mom at the age of twenty-one. I was dejected, depressed, and determined never to let another woman break my heart again.

At nineteen, TJ moved out of state and got married. He and his wife now have four children, and they are doing well. Having experienced life as part of two broken homes and growing up without my biological father, it was important to me that TJ always knew I would never quit being his dad, no matter what.

Today, I'm a proud granddad. I strive to instill love, passion, and compassion in my grandchildren, encouraging them to make thoughtful decisions. I hope and pray that their choices are consistent and that they always consider how their words and actions affect others.

When Terry Met Donna

I was introduced to Donna in September 1982 by our now-dearest friend, Ranetta, whom I had met while working at Harris Trust and Savings Bank in downtown Chicago. I had been working there since 1978, starting right after high school at Harris's 311 West Monroe building. When our team transferred to Harris's 111 West Monroe building, I felt isolated because all my friends were still at 311. However, it was only two blocks away, so I managed to adjust.

Donna was incredibly well-liked by her coworkers, unlike anyone I had ever seen. Even Ranetta told me how Donna's positivity inspired her to remain hopeful during the worst of times. Donna's life outside of work, however, was a mystery to me. I knew only one thing: I wanted to know more about her. When she invited me to her birthday party in 1982, I made sure to attend. Like most people going to a house party for the first time, I brought a friend with me—my long-time buddy, Al. Together, we headed to Donna's house at 23rd and Ridgeway Streets on Chicago's West Side, in the Lawndale community.

To my surprise, instead of dancing, drinking, and smoking, the party revolved around playing cards. Unfortunately, Al didn't play cards and quickly grew bored. Being the good friend that I am, I drove him back to Bronzeville and then returned to the party to join the card games.

At the time, I was in a relationship, and so was Donna. But that night, we played cards until 5:00 a.m. and ended the morning with a trip to White Castle for burgers and fries, the only place open that served more than breakfast at that hour. During my time at Harris Bank, I started playing cards during lunch breaks with Donna and her friends. Our groups of friends became close, and soon we were having card parties at each other's homes, creating unforgettable memories.

Donna started taking an interest in me, which was both surprising and exciting. At that point, I had already decided she was the one for me. When she asked me out on a date—not as a boyfriend, but as coworkers wanting to know each other better—I jumped at the chance. Our first date was at the Miami Bowling Center on 49th and Pulaski Streets in Chicago. Donna was an avid bowler, having started at sixteen, and since I wanted to spend time with her, I pretended to love bowling too. I even joined the Harris bowling league just to be around her. Sneaky, right?

As we grew closer, we started spending more time together, leaving less time for anyone else, including our previous relationships. Six months later, we decided to make it official and became a couple. The first member of her family I met was her father, Earl. For a man who grew up without a biological father, meeting hers felt like a blessing. Earl was laid-back and cool—completely opposite of Donna's hardworking and straightforward mom, Donnie, whom I met later. Donna clearly inherited her best qualities from both parents.

Donna asked me to move into her home in 1982. At first, I hesitated because of my previous experience moving in with a woman, and because she lived with her elderly parents. Her mom initially disapproved of her "unorthodox" decision. But Donna stood her ground, saying, "Well, we'll just move to Oak Park, IL then!" That was all the assurance I needed to move in.

In November 1985, one day after Thanksgiving and three and a half years of "testing" each other, we decided to make it official and got engaged. By that time, we were already a committed couple. On June 14, 1986, on a hot, muggy day, we got married at Blessed Sacrament Church. I used to joke that my last decision as a free man was saying, "I do." Donna doesn't find that funny—not one bit!

Our wedding was huge, with 250 guests (twenty-five of whom were mine). The colors were pink and gray, and the wedding party included twenty people. Since we had already been living together as husband and wife with Donna's parents, our honeymoon was in—you guessed it—Oak Park, IL! We stayed at a local hotel, Pleasant, located on Randolph and Marion Streets. It was just five miles west of downtown Chicago, and we spent the entire weekend in the room.

In 1991, after eight years living on the West Side, we moved into a Georgian-style home in Bellwood, IL, eight miles west of downtown Chicago, where we've lived ever since.

For twenty-five years, Donna never took a sick day. Meanwhile, I took sick days for everything from dandruff to hangnails to the flu. When she began to fall ill in 2012, little did I know how much our lives would change. Now, twelve years later, I've been a full-time caregiver and a full-time employee at a large insurance company for thirty-seven years. Transitioning from husband to husband/caregiver has been challenging but rewarding. It has given me purpose, stability, and a responsibility not to quit on Donna.

Donna is a huge fan of our South Side baseball team—a love she inherited from her father. She's incredibly athletic and has excelled in softball, basketball, volleyball, and especially bowling. In fact, she bowled a perfect 300 on August 4, 2001. My bowling teams, on the other hand, were so bad they barely wanted me on the roster.

Despite my missed opportunities, bad decisions, and even being a quitter at times, Donna chose me. She picked me despite my faults—having a son at twenty, having no money, and even losing my job for a year. Donna once said something that still resonates with me today: "If I can't be with you when you're down, then I don't want to be with you at all."

Recently, I asked her, "WHY DID YOU PICK ME?"

She joked, "BECAUSE YOU HAD A LOT OF MONEY!" What a liar! The truth, as she later admitted, was that despite my faults, she saw someone willing to work hard to get better. She met me while I was working and attending college, and she didn't want just any man—she wanted *her* man.

And she got him—Me!

I once found an old survey in one of Donna's magazines about what she thought of her husband. One question asked, "How would you rate your husband?" Her answer: "Nine." Even ten years later, I'm still a nine, and I'm perfectly okay with that. I don't want to be a perfect husband—I just want to be a *good, honest, and loving* one.

Living Life as a Comedian

"Life can feel like one big joke with many punchlines. Learning to recognize what's funny and embracing it is key.

What seemed impossible in 2012 turned into a blessing by 2024. I pray, cry, adjust, love, understand, and support. Donna and I are still together as one. Most people refer to us as soulmates.

Donna and I are two versions of the same person.

As the legendary artist Prince sings in his song *Adore*: "Love is too weak to define what you mean to me."

What we have is a blessing from God, and we've learned that "quitting is not an option" and "nothing is impossible until it's done."

The End

Milton Keynes UK
Ingram Content Group UK Ltd.
UKHW041330301124
451950UK00020B/173/J